Uncharted Dreams

By

Jade Kornegay

Copyrights

Title: Uncharted Dreams
Published by: Chipper Publications
Copyright: © 2008 Matthew Haynes/Aislinn Audrina Kornegay
ISBN: 978-0-6151-9769-2

Dedication

To my mother, thank you for passing down your passion for writing, my love of life, and my ability to put them together.

To my husband whose enthusiasm and faith in me has pushed me into my success.

About The Author

Jade Kornegay was born in the small town of Brewster Washington and is now residing in Belleville Illinois with her husband and two beautiful children. She graduated from Webster University with a degree in political science with an emphasis in public law. Jade says about this book, "Writing with emotion and passion is very important to me. Poetry is something very personal and I hope that this book touches many hearts." Jade's website is www.jadekornegay.com. Be looking for more from Jade in the near future.

A Message

The time is near,
And soon He will be coming,
To gather His flock.
His precious little lambs,
Who have been persecuted for Him,
Who have worn His name
and spread it all throughout the land.

Do not fear,
He is and always will be—
With you.
He has sent you to harvest His grain.
O' hand out His bread,
Quench every man's thirst.
Quickly gather every seed you can,
And sign it over to Him in blood.

A Poem

When you came into my life,
The sun shined brighter,
The eagles soared higher.
Our love is as one,
Like Romeo and Juliet.
We are bound together,
Once again by the dagger.
When your love for me grows cold,
I shall be like that of a single rose,
Whose life has been taken,
By someone who cares no more.

Addicted to You

I have never met you,
Yet I know all about you.
Staring into your deep eyes,
I listen to your soothing accented voice.
Feeling your soft and warm skin,
I caress your sandy brown hair.
Your large and slender hands,
Embrace me close to you.

Everything about you is something,
I just cannot live without.
When it comes to you I feel like such a lush.
I am addicted to you;
As you are the man I love.

All of You

All you do,
Is all that you should do.
Where you are,
Is where you should be.
What you say,
Is what you should say.
All of you,
Is all that you should be—
YOU!

Amove-Ero

The times remembered,
When we were together; Amovero.

You were so happy,
A glimmer in your eyes; Amoveris.

Then one of us had to leave,
You saw I must be strong; Amoverit.

Behold the Beauty

Rolling in like the thunder,
Crashing against the rocks,
With fury and rage it screams,
While we walk the docks.

People see romanticism,
A place to find love,
Leaving footprints in the sand.
Tides bring life to the shore,
Then leave it on the land.

To truly see its mysterious beauty,
You have to stare into the deep.
Once you are under,
Your love will slowly creep.

Heed to my warning,
And proceed with caution,
For it is treacherous.

It is swift and strong,
It can easily take your life,
For it is not afraid of us.

Boy Meets Girl

There once was a young girl,
Who walked through the dense forest.
The trees so very high,
And everything so very wild,
Especially in the month of May.

She walked for hours studying everything,
Failing to notice she had caught her sweater,
And that it had begun to tear away.
Half way through the forest,
She realized she was lost.
Gathering dark from the faded light;
She was losing sight of the day.

She was scared and alone in the dark,
All she could do was rest and pray
She could not die here in this forest,
She would find a tree and underneath she would lie.

Along came a gentleman hunter of sorts.
Spotting some string, he followed the way.
Curious about where it would lead,
He followed a long time wondering if it stopped at the bay.

Following this trail of string along a deer's path,
He lost sight of it because of its fray.
He stumbled across someone's dirt tracks,
And some curds from their whey.

Wise and always true to his self,
He knew not to himself he would betray.
Faster and faster he moved onward,
Thinking of how the adventure made him joyous and gay.

There she lay sleeping when he came upon her.
He stood wondering what to say,
Amazed by her beauty so vivid.

Golden hair, full lips, eyes of green,
Her face as soft as a doll made of clay.

He went over and tapped her shoulder;
She awoke and said, "What is this day?"
Her voice was like harps and his like trumpets.
He answered not but thought, "Just one day."

They began talking and found their way home.
He fell in love in an instant,
And was begging her to stay.
She had grown fond but wanted to take some time,
So she simply answered, "one day."

Off they went together into the sunset,
With the sky as gold as a straw of hay.
Hand in hand with smiles so big,
They walked happily ever after,
Together forever and always!

Crush

I see you sitting over there, I smile.
You look at me and return,
My gesture with a smile.
I think about you all the time.
How would I get the nerve to call,
Even if I did have a dime?
I will admit that I think your pants are nicely fit,
Sometimes I wish they would split.
Of course I will never tell,
What I think or how I feel.
Every time you wink,
My heart is what you steal.
I do believe it to be for the best,
That I do not tell the rest.
The fact is I am glad you are there,
Waiting to give me that warming stare.
Whenever I feel down and out,
Just one glance makes my heart shout.
I see you sitting there across the room,
As you look up and give me a big smile.
You make my day, you make me laugh.
You make me feel so different
When I am alone in thought,
There is only you and me.

Cry Baby

Cry,
Baby Barbarino cries one single tear,
Everyday just one single tear.
A rebel whose parents were killed,
As a promise, a tear a day.

Cry,
Baby Barbarino sad and weak.
Full of life, he has no family—
Just his friends.

Dedication to You

I was awakened by the phone ringing,
I picked up the receiver,
And a man started singing.
As five and ten minutes passed by,
I found myself just sitting there,
With the receiver to my ear.

Enjoying the sweet songs of love,
Every melody and chord he was singing.
The music continued for a while,
I got lost in the moment.

He finally stopped and said "hello".
I paused for a brief moment,
Realizing I didn't know who he was.
In a zone I simply, quickly replied "Hi".

He told me who he was,
And why he called.
Then of course came a joke.
It was really silly,
I couldn't contain myself.

He laughed and said,
"I had a great laugh."
After conversing for many hours,
Meeting each other and spending everyday together,
Love came and still remains.

Dream

He is the one in my dream,
I dreamt so many years ago.
I prayed to God to send me love,
You came along and at a glance I knew,
My dearest God has sent me you.

I should have told you how I felt,
How you were the one for me.
Instead I let you slip through my fingers,
Like a grain of sand sifting to the ground.

Wondering if there is still hope,
I would have to say I do not know.
Then again as of late,
That seems to be the answer,
To all my questions.

Emptiness

You see the world as a deep dark place,
Of unimaginable death and gloom.
Shadows are being the bride,
And evil her groom.

There are things that withhold the power,
To tempt your unforeseen fate.
Leading you to and past the forbidden gate,
Something with such power over the human mind,
Are all the evil and none the kind.

With the dark angel Lucifer,
You have made a pact.
Forget about turning around,
For there is no looking back.
A promise has been written,
With your own blood and pain.
Your soul shall never be free,
From the horrid scarlet stain.

Do you want your soul to return free?
You must make Lucifer bow down upon his knee.
"How?" you ask, "How do I accomplish this deed?"
Fill his eyes with a light as bright as the sun,
Then my friend your deed will be done.

Every

Every time I see you walk by,
I turn around for second glances.
Things begin to look fuzzy;
And seem to run in slow motion.
Dreams of our secret romances,
Scamper in a recalling fantasy.

I do not really know you,
Only your name and that you like to dance.
Across the room each in our corners,
Who will make the move?
Will it sting?

I want to talk to you but all I can say is "Hi."
I feel so foolish and silly.
Every minute since the first day we met,
I have been thinking about stealing a kiss.
Maybe I should take a breath,
Be brave and take my chances.
If luck turns into fate we go to the floor,
So you can hold me close while my heart dances.

Fierce

Like a sunset in a darkening sky at days end,
Her eyes of gold seemed to glow…fierce.
Quick and lively her reflexes are like no other,
Her abilities daily do grow…fierce.
Sexy, feminine, lovely, independent to say the least,
She is without a doubt…fierce.
Misunderstood and secure a cat woman,
A friendly feline beast…fierce.
Like a stalker in the night,
She prowls the blackness,
Watching and waiting…fierce.
With her womanly influence,
You will find it is her prey,
She is baiting…fierce.

Forsaken

Why have your forsaken me,
My love for you was so strong.
With you is where my heart shall be,
Always and forever belong.
You made me feel as though a dagger,
Had pierced my very soul.
Maybe my heart is bleeding,
Because you shot it with a bow.
You said that you loved me,
And that you truly did care.
It is good I know your dirty traits,
You just thought I was unaware.
I hope your lust has made you happy,
For my broken heart has shattered.
From ashes to ashes and dust to dust,
I will never forgive you like that of Romeo and Juliet.
Maybe we should have thought ahead,
And jumped over a safety net.
You have lied and left my body,
To be stripped by the ghettos.
My body rained and snowed upon,
Pierced by the beaks of wild crows.
My spirit and the undying memory of my love,
Shall haunt your days forever;
Making you push that final shove.

God's Song

Hey ya'll I'm the new girl in town,
Better get to know me cuz' I'm stickin' around.
Listen up, I'm gonna try and teach ya,
I've got a message from the man,
He's really tryin' to reach ya.

The time is near to gather His flock,
He's commin' down don't be shocked.
You'll know it's that time,
When you hear the trumpet sound.

We bear His name,
We spread His word,
His spirit soars above us like a bird.
The precious little lambs,
Living all about the ground,
Listen to these words,
With Jesus you wont be wound.

Just use your brain,
And gather His grain,
For all you have to do is claim His name.
Feed everyone the word,
Free them from being bound.
Quench every man's thirst,
And secure their crown.

Heart

Reach into that vast pit of emptiness,
Where your soul clearly lies..
Tell it to forgive me,
Tell it how much I care.
Call into it, "remember, I love you."
And wait for it to reply.
Give it wings to help it lighten,
For burdens must weigh it down.
Surround it with warmth,
So that it won't get cold.
Fill it with fine sugar,
So it won't become bitter.
Admire it as I do,
Look at its great complexity.
Shower it with love to help it grow,
To inspiring proportions.
Remind it of all the good,
So that it will broaden its memory.
Be sure to wish it well,
May it never break and shatter.

Him

There is something so wonderful about him.
Every time he smiles it seems as though time slows,
Or his deep voice lingering in the air for hours and days.
The way he smells when he wraps you in his strong arms,
Makes his presence very well known.
There is something so distinguished about him.
His lips curl around his perfect smile,
While he laughs with his whole body.
He wrinkles his forehead in deep thought,
Setting off his serious side.
There is something so sensual about him,
Like the way he bites his bottom lip,
When curiosity overpowers him.
The way he looks deeply into your eyes,
Makes you feel extremely faint.
The way he makes you long for him and ache for him,
There is something about him.

Honky Tonk Count

Nine, Eight, Seven, Six, Two by Four,
Big ol' Chevy with four on the floor.
Going to my baby doll's house tonight,
Pray'n that there's not another in sight.
Gonna play a game of poker and drink me a beer,
Getting this party into second gear.
I'm coming home with the riding sun,
But not a minute before I'm done.
You could call it love but don't be too sure,
Life is coming back with that same ol' blur.

How I See It

As summer ends and fall begins,
Bright yellow, orange and brown leaves fall to the ground.
I look around and think about your dark eyes,
Creamy chocolate drops of sweetness and kindness.

The coolness in the fall air makes me excited,
To feel your warm and gentle embrace,
And welcome your soft, handsome face.
As long as time goes on,
And the sun rises making a new dawn,
Nothing can ever change the way I feel.
It is with you where I belong.

You indulge my every need,
You are the one that believes.
Like the moon to the river,
We always conceive the brightest glimmer.

From east to west and north to south,
There is no need we should ever have doubt.
Only a love as strong as ours will stay,
As bright as the nearest stars.
The warmth of our hearts and sparks in our soul,
Together always but will never grow old.

I've Never Known Love

I don't believe I have ever known love,
Until this very day.
So confused and feeling so strange,
For the very first time.
Twenty-four seven all I think about is you.
My heart beats so wildly,
And my eyes look so passionately.
I think you feel the same way,
You certainly put on the face.
Will we spend eternity together?
I have to tell if you don't know already—
I Love You.
Wondering how much love is worth,
What are the extents a person would endure for love?
Whenever I am around you,
I just melt on the spot.
The feeling gets stranger as we go,
Throughout each minute,
I will be sitting there pondering,
About what you're doing.

I Want What I Want

I am a very simple person;
I try not to ask too much.
Not too much of a hopeful romantic,
There have only been a few things I always wanted.
I want to be an inspiration to the man that loves me.
A poem, a love letter, an act of complete compulsion,
And someone to dance in the rain with,
Or walk hand in hand with.
Playing put-put golf and not afraid to be kid,
Even having someone to go to the drive-in with.
Someone who covers me up and lies beside me,
When I fall asleep on the floor.
One who calls me just because,
pops in for a bite, walks me to my car.
If this is too much to ask then so be it.

If I Could

If I could I would make you a shield,
To protect you from harm coming your way.
If I could I would make you an iron dress,
To put around your softened heart,
Protecting you from love that is blind.
If I could I would make you a happy life,
Full of sweet bliss to protect you from reality.
If I could I would write you a story,
To protect you from realism,
So that you might see this world as a story—
If only I could.

In Jesus' Name

In Jesus' grace I live each day.
In Jesus' footsteps I try and stay.
On the paths of the straight and narrow,
He leads the way.
In Jesus' arms I feel safe.
In Jesus' love I have a place.
No worry, no debts, I have no regrets.
In Jesus' word I learn life's secrets.
In Jesus' presence I feel his pull,
For in Jesus' death I am paid in full.

Indulgence

A look,
Mesmerizing,
Heart racing,
Skin flushed,
Left wanting more.

A kiss,
Tantalizing,
Sweat dripping,
Muscles tightening,
Breathing begins to stagger.

A touch,
Electrifying,
Hair raising,
Lips plump,
Body hot to touch—
Pure Ecstasy.

John

He is almost my most beloved loved-one.
I follow him here,
I follow him there,
I would follow him anywhere.
John is big and brave, and strong,
Yet he hurts when he puts aftershave on.
He is cool, charming, and sweet,
But boy you should watch him eat.
He is an all around kind of guy,
Who would help just about anyone.
No matter how cool, charming, sweet, big, brave or strong,
He will always be number one.

<u>Passage John 3:16</u>

As I walk down a dark alley,
I see in a shadowed corner a small orphan.
I took him home and cleaned him up,
Showed him the way, and called him my own.
He has graduated from college and hates everyone,
He shows absolutely no feeling for anyone.
"Waste of time!" He says while smirking.

I told him the story of Jesus' birth and death,
I read aloud passage John 3:16.
"For God so loved the world that he gave His only begotten son that who so ever believeth in Him shall not perish but have ever lasting life."

All of a sudden I saw a sparkle in his eyes,
When he started to cry we hugged and said, "I Love You".
He surprised me by following with, "And I always will."

Just Met

We've only just met and yet I feel,
As though I've known you forever.
Every time I look into your eyes,
I feel tingling all over.
I love spending time with you;
If I could only be with you every day.
You're sweet and kind,
Soon you'll be all mine.
I think about you twenty-four seven,
The complete before, during, and after.
I have never known anyone like this,
And thought I never would.
Could it be true love,
Catching my heart on fire?
Maybe its love that fills my stomach with knots.
I love talking to you, glancing at you, flirting with you.
I love touching, kissing, and being around you.

Kisses

Please, I beg you to kiss me just once,
So it feels like an eternity,
Like a thousand kisses.
Fulfill all of my passionate wishes,
Then kiss me again and like the first let it be.
Beautiful and shimmering like the deep blue sea,
Keep it tender and gentle, very flirtatious.
All the sweetness, lick your lips, it's so delicious.
It is love at first sight;
You are the one for me.
Those who believe in destiny and fate,
Love can be so hard to find.
You my love are the one for me,
My eternal mate.
Have you ever seen the golden gate?
Don't worry love is kind if not sublime.

Lambert

A man so beautiful,
So full of life,
Worthy of a good woman's love.
What makes a man worthy?
I can not say,
I am not the woman.
For me he shall be tall with dark hair,
Green eyes, healthy and passionate.
He must be nice, good humored, and romantic.
He is very intelligent and witty,
Someone that will always treat me right.
Is there such a man? Shall we ever meet?
Is he trustworthy? What does he want?

Leaves

Have you ever seen a leaf fall from a tree,
Kissed gently by the breeze,
And falling into the water floating endlessly—
Endlessly?

Where,
I do not know.
Then as it starts to rain,
It is touched by raindrops,
Falling from up high.
At times I wish I were that leaf,
Floating onward to a place I do not know.

Lost Restraint

You know not what you ask of me,
Together forever you want us to be.
A protest I must state.
You have made your decision too quick,
To be with me I must be like a thorn,
And your finger I must prick.
The cost is far too great.
Here I am before you, caressing you neck.
I can feel your heart begin to rush.
Your skin so beautiful and warm,
I love to make it blush.
On my shoulder would be immense self-hate.
I can feel the hunger rage at this midnight hour.
Leave me until I can regain my will power.
Hurry now before it is too late.
Kissing your lips a little too passionately,
Your lips bleed so salty sweet.
I must control myself,
This hunger I must beat.
I cannot allow this to be your fate.
My love, my sweet darling,
It is time for you to go.
I will not be the one to make you grow cold.
Go now, away for a while,
Do as you are told!

Mine

Oh my baby, my smiling baby,
My delicate baby, you are so unknowing,
So full of curiosity and life.

Oh my child, my beautiful child,
My wild child, you are so warm and caring.
You stretch your boundaries; try to conquer the world,
And fly with your towel flapping behind you.

Oh my young adult, my proud young adult,
My eager young adult, you have passions unknown,
And desires like those of your ancestors.

Oh my baby all grown up, so handsome,
So brave, you have accomplished your goals.
You have fulfilled your destiny,
You have made me so proud.

<u>My Song</u>

You wake up each morning with a smile on your face,
And look around seeing nothing but an empty space.
Turn; turn around and in one single place,
Wondering what you're missing,
Someone to be kissing.

Where's the one I'm meant for,
Someone to warm my heart?
The one to say "I love you, I have from the start."
Walking down the walkways together,
My hand in yours.

You stop and so gently put your face in your hands,
Crying so meekly but drowning so deeply.
Looking out the window, nothing to be found,
The entire world around you turning always—
Upside down.

People walking by you stop just to stare,
No one stops to talk, and no one even cares.
Searching desperately for someone's life to share,
Walking down the highway together forever,
My hand in yours.

Who am I?
Where is he?
Is it meant to be?
My only God I pray to,
You let my dreams become a reality.

Send the one I am meant to be with,
Send him here to me.
Traveling each way looking up every tree,
Let us be together forever in eternity.
Never let our love go cold,
Together we shall grow old.

Forever locked in sanctity,
We walk, my hand in yours.

Oh, her

I once knew a girl,
She claimed to be queen.
I'm not quite sure how,
For she was very mean.

She had curly hair,
It was long and blond.
Yet she smelled up the room,
With the scent of "Goldbond".

Then there was a handsome boy,
Who thought he could be any girl's sex toy.
He was blond and had bright blue eyes,
To the majority of women so do most guys.
As you can see it is no surprise,
Life turned out the way it did,
She got pregnant and he went and hid.

Now all alone, fat and scared,
She had no place to run, no place to hide.
He is no longer blessed and dignified.
There's the end of my story,
I hope you received my message.
Even though you're seventeen or eighteen,
And made a prom queen,
Beauty is not always glory!

One-Two-Three-All

Sometimes when you look across the night waters,
You don't even have to look up at the sky.
Complete calmness, you can barely hear the wind blow by.
That is not life, not in the least,
Day by day growing stranger like a beast.
Not resting, never sleeping, and always tearing away at your soul,
Until one or the other is deceased.
Look up at the sky and stretch your arms out,
Spin and spin until you can't spin anymore.
Laying there straight and narrow along the river shore,
This is what life is about, all three put together and combined.
It will always be as thus, there is no way around.
Be still and watch the compassion grow over time.

Our World

Rape, murder, sex, drugs, foul language,
And television advertisements everywhere.
These are some of the things happening in our towns,
And all across our streets.
The lists of victims,
Millions of pages long.

Lock your doors; shut your windows tight,
Keep yourself safe even though it shuts you off,
From the rest of the world.
Don't live like this, in fear.
Stand up to your government,
Write letters and make calls.
Save our world.

Pride

Our Pride,
Our Dignity,
Our Heritage,
Our Memories.

My people were a happy people,
We did not know of such things,
As disease or modern problems.
We had no need for money, or greed!
You came with greed in your heart,
And fully on your minds.
You took our land, our families,
And our way of life.
You gave us disease,
You left us starving.
You put us into small camps,
With no room to breath.
You tried to make slaves out of us,
As we slipped away you said we were no good.
One thing you have never stolen,
And never will is our pride.

Put Forth

Put forth thine hand and feel,
The warmth of the golden sun.
Thou now have warmth as well as light.
Thine kindest thoughts like the day have begun,
Lasting forever with pure and simple delight.
Roll in the darkness,
Along with the clouds.
Sudden bursts of electricity,
Flashes in thine eyes.
As the cold rain pours down upon thine body,
And thine breaths become seen.

Real Love

I see him, or do I?
I see all the pain,
But that isn't him.
I see his long, hard, trying life,
His dark secrets and sad memories,
But that isn't him.
So how do I see him?

I see wrinkles on his forehead when he is sorry,
The dimples so round as he smiles.
I see the tears slowly run down his slender face.
I see how his curiosity gets him into trouble,
And how quick wit and charm get him out of it.
I see his tongue loll around his perfect teeth,
Creating his slightly accented voice.
I see how his hands feel with a gentle touch,
How his eyes, so big, wander constantly,
As if seeing everything for the first time.
I see him,
I adore him,
I will always love him.

Real World

People watch movies and try to live like them.
They try to be perfect;
Try to live like the stars do.
There is a reason it doesn't work.
Movies are dreams, not reality!
Just because they have realistic ideas,
Does not make them doable.
Movies are too contradictory,
Love is good, love hurts.
Friends are always there for you,
Friends aren't always there.
Why do people fall for it?
The world is a dream.

Roaming

Roaming around in each others thoughts,
Finger tips caressing lips ever so gently.
Looking into the depths as dark as midnight,
Our souls emerging so intimately.
I loved when we spent all night,
Dancing in the parking lot.
Then you took me,
And stole my heart so quickly.

Smiley

My dearest friend that just turned sixteen,
Could bend in all ways without breaking her spleen.
Here I am to explain the unseen.
She loves to love men I am sure,
She has fifty in her den,
For that disease we have no cure.
Through the thick and thin,
We will always have within,
The men we both share without a care.
She had poofy hair and the guys all stare,
But when she is done they all have to run,
Because of her deeds they are all of seeds.
Their buckles undone shows the amount of fun.
When the sun goes down you can see her crown,
With spotted jewels and no time for renewals.
A hard day of work with Dave the jerk,
And a few of his friends who all wear depends.
In log cabins you should see what happens,
On a bench which isn't a cinch.
As I once said about my dear friend,
Who just turned sweet sixteen.
You all have proof that she can bend,
In all ways without breaking her spleen.

So Wise

You think you are so wise,
Because you have survived,
Because you are evil.
You kill here to ask you,
Why you do what you do,
And take whatever you want.
You actually think you deserve it.

Tell me,
Do you deserve it because you are special?
Is it because you are you?
You are a liar and a thief,
A scoundrel and a murderer.

You show no remorse yet you are full of regret,
Your conscience yelling at you.
Now I am here to ask you why,
Do you do what you do?
Why do you think you have that right?

Like everyone else, do the crime do the time.
Millions of others have gone through the same.
If you stop and think you will see,
There is no one else to blame except the guilty.

Song or Sand

Singing is a talent, a way of expressing yourself,
A way of releasing what is inside, an art.
There are many great people that love to sing,
But that is not enough.
There is enthusiasm but where is the meaning?

Those sole diamonds amongst the stars,
Do not just love to sing, they sing with love.
If you do not sing with love,
There will always remain a barrier or gap.
It can only be filled by simple passion.

When you accomplish this life long goal,
You will be noticed by many and loved by all.
Your voice will float above the clouds,
And all around each grain of sand.

Sun, Moon, Stars = Eclipse

There was a story from long ago,
Told from generation to generation.
It was said that in the beginning of time,
There was nothing but darkness.
The creator took the largest pearl from the sea,
And placed it perfect in the sky.
From then on it was known as Mother Moon.
One day, after Mother Moon had prayed for a partner;
The Creator took a cinder from his burning pool and threw it into the sky.
From then on he was known as Father Sun.
Even though Father Sun was sent to meet her,
He spent many years chasing Mother Moon.
Every night Mother Moon would leave a diamond for Father Sun to find,
To show that he retrieved it, Father Sun left two more in its place.
Finally one day they really met,
Joining these two created an eclipse.
Stars burst and shot across the sky,
Leaving trails of sparks miles behind them.
And so it has been ever since,
And so it shall always be.

Thanks to Love

Every time I look around the corner,
I find another problem.
For some reason I can't find anyone that loves me,
As much as I love them.
Always trying to reach out to them,
Always trying to learn more about them.
Always trying to hold onto something,
I never even had.
Does love exist?
Did it just become a human dream,
Laid of perfection and happiness?
I am tired of all the excuses,
And all the lies I have heard.
Perhaps it is time to quit;
I have no trust or faith left.
Thanks to love,
I have complete emptiness.

The Days Are Going By Fast

The days are going by fast and everything looks new. When I fell in love, my dear, I fell in love with you. This feeling is new to me and seems like a lifelong deal. Sometimes I lay and think if this is for real. I'm not sure how I'm supposed to act. My love for you is a well-known fact that all can see. A love that is never ending is one I can abide by. It's one to reveal, not to bury and hold deep inside.

The days are going by fast and I'm in love with you. Love is the way you feel and not something you can steal. A real high score for passion you raked. The farther along, higher and higher it began to stack. When trouble comes near, you're always by my side. This proves the fact I have relied heavily on you.

The days are going by quickly now and I will never leave you. When I pass away, my dear, I hope regret will never find you. You have my heart, my soul, and my mind. When I am with you there is no space or even time. When we grow old our love will still feel new. So you see I did not lie, my dear, when I said that I love you.

The River Of Us

You flow so gentle tinkling down the curves,
In an instant you burst and twist rapidly.
Have you ever compared me to yourself?
You would see we are much alike.
Only my downward direction is like your life,
With calm spots, shallow spots, and rough spots.
Low seasons, high seasons, some areas full of life,
And some with almost none.
I make people very happy,
Yet I can bring fear to anyone.
I can be stopped and helpless,
Or overflow and deadly.

Thrive

Tis' the night of the living,
And thou art both mine moon and stars.
To turn thine glowing face away from thee,
Would cause an eclipse for eternity.
Whisper ten thousand beautiful things,
Fill mine ears with joy and happiness.
Whilst thou intertwine thine heart with my soul?
In thought, caress every tenderness,
With a simple stare and a glance of passion.
Show thine inners as well as thine outers,
Show them whole to me.
The deadliest of weapons to all living creatures—
Tis' love.
Only those with the truest hearts,
Shall conquer all.
Thine quest should thrive to be the one,
In thine self where thou art.
Hiding, seeking, wanting to be, not fall,
To you forever my love you can call.

Transformation

I was lost at one time in a place,
We will call denial.
Every time I looked at me,
I saw the person I used to be.
Life brought new struggles and fears,
Little joy and many tears.
There were many who warned me,
Of what I would soon see.
A simple photograph,
A frozen moment in time.
Finally I saw who I had become,
No longer recognizable, I had lost me.
Surely I had to be somewhere trapped inside,
Screaming to be set free.
There were many trials, many failures,
And so many disappointments.
I couldn't let go again,
I might not be able to find me a second time.
Through all the good and bad times,
I found the mountain I had to climb.
On the journey we began one transformation,
Painful was the process,
There are still scars that remain.
The end result was beyond comparison,
I finally found the person I used to be,
I finally found me!

What?

I find myself very confused,
It seems as though,
All my friends have been rewired.
My dear friend Jared tried to kill himself,
Joy got into a car accident,
And everyone has turned against Dawn.
Still I don't see the point,
Of doing any of that stuff.
Then I realized that I fell in love,
With a real cowboy.
He is sweet, handsome, brave, and strong.
When I met him I knew,
He was the one for me.
Hopefully that won't change,
Through the years.

Why

Now you return to me?
After the many months we were apart?
Through all of those many months,
I sat and wondered why it didn't work out.
I wondered if you did or did not care,
What would've happened if we could've worked it out?
Why did you say you love me,
Only to change your mind and not take a risk?

Now you want me to forget al about it,
Forgive you; take you back in my arms.
I don't know if I can.
I loved you so much I would've done anything for you,
I would've taken any risk.
When I start to actually get over you,
You come back along with all the memories and feelings.

You are handsome, kind, warm, and gentle.
I loved to be with you.
I remember us driving around,
You were singing along with the radio.
I ran my fingers through your hair,
As you looked into my eyes,
And every time I would melt.

Everybody was against us.
Even though we've gone through a great deal,
With a horrible break up, I forgive you.
I can never stay mad as long as you realize,
Things will never be as they were.

Are you playing tricks with my mind?
Are you trying to confuse me?
Are you going to lie to me again?
Only time will tell.
For the future generations ahead,

Let me share as I will,
With you my earned wisdom,
That love does not—
    Conquer all.

Window

Look out the window,
See the changes of season begin.
From spring to fall the leaves change colors,
The sight of your breath present.
From fall to winter you see people bundled up,
The trees all bare, snow on the distant mountains.
Winter to spring, the birds start chirping,
The grass is green, heavy with the smell of dew.
Spring to summer the sun shines bright and hot,
The water is warm and the beaches full of sand.
Look out your window and see the people change,
The cities change, and the world change.

Wolf

In the depths of the forest I stand alone,
Yet echoing throughout the forest is a wild howl,
Almost sounding like some sort of song.

With lightning speed you surround me.
Your eyes with a deep cold stare,
Send my heart to thumping.
With a mouth full of fangs you grow,
You wear me down with your razor sharp claws,
You are the most dangerous of predators.

World

I don't see the world as a place I want to be.
The clouds are moving faster as if they were breaking free.

More and more people are filling up this place,
Taking up all the land.
Living wherever they can,
Leaving the world a disgrace.

The weather is changing,
There are many more storms.
Driving people against people,
Making even children bare arms.

I don't see the world as a place I want to be,
Everything is dying and polluted,
There is nothing here to see.

Very soon I shall rise to a place of grace,
Where I shall see my Lord and savior's shining face.

You Knew

I was born into the light,
Managing to stay faithful for years.
Then things started to change,
My life turned upside down.
I knew I was in the wrong,
But talked myself out of doing anything.
Looking behind me,
I pictured tears falling from the heavens.

Ashamed,
Almost to the point of no return,
Was my direction.
A voice from the heavens,
Sounded through the sky.
"I love you, do not shed my light,
I am all forgiving,
Purify thyself and look at me for your answers,
For your needs."
Here I am now whole,
Completed and totally adored.
The only love I ever needed,
Was one I should have been looking for,
The everlasting love of God.

You Know Who You Are

To see you smile is like seeing the sun surround my body,
With shimmering golden rays of warmth.
To run my fingers through you hair is like feeling the wind,
Brush past my hand ever so gently.
To hear you laugh is like dancing in the rain,
Making me feel fresh, alive and free.
To look into your eyes is like staring up at the night sky,
Deep and mysterious, sparkling no matter what.
Whenever we are together we are always laughing and smiling.
You are my best friend through thick and thin,
There is no time for slacking.
When I am with you I feel as though I can fly,
Soaring with great speed, high above in the sky.
We share a love like no other you will ever see,
Friends forever; together we shall be.
Someday I will tell you how I feel,
Until that day my gut I shall not spill.

Tuff

My best friend is turning sixteen;
She wanted to be a rodeo queen.
I learned from her the trick of the trade,
As I got older I got better with it every day.

One day she turned to me and said:

"I'm passing on what I know so I can go to the man I love. He's not real rich, he's not all that, but his heart is good and I'm wearing his hat. I can't keep playing this game my hunting grounds are not the same. They used to call me the rodeo queen I had every man I needed to keep me warm and love me all night but now my heart is starting to fight. I need to leave with title in-tact so here you go take my rodeo hat. Be safe, be strong, I know you'll find someone to sing a song with. So until we meet again you remain a true friend. Look up don't close your eyes to my rodeo queen I say good bye."

I haven't seen her since,
But she still remains the rodeo queen.

Bum

    Have you ever made fun of someone just to look good in front of your so called "friends"? Everyone does it sooner or later, but have you ever wondered about how that might affect the other person? Maybe you've been made fun of for being poorer or less fortunate than others. Let's say you run your own business but the person you have to pay rent to treats you like less than dirt.

    Now think of the unfortunate people that live in cardboard boxes, in dumpsters, under bridges, and in bushes. Do you ever wonder what happened to them? What might their story be? Perhaps they were abandoned on the streets at a fairly young age and were not lucky enough to be taken in. With no education, no friends, and no job, what would you do?. With no family, no money, and no food, where would you go? No clothes, no shopping, and no holiday celebrations, how would you feel?

    These victims may have lost everything in a fire and put them in a poor mental state. It is possible they couldn't rebound from their tragedy.. There is a possibility that their family member got into an accident. This may be because that individual was driving drunk after getting fired from their job. The end result may have been killing everyone and leaving the victim alone. Not being able to pay for funeral costs, they take everything away. Instead they bury themselves in their own anguish and give up all hope of starting over.

    Do you serve your country well? Just say there was a man on the streets in the freezing cold with no legs, sitting in his wheelchair. He had been through a war to protect our country, but you don't know that. You didn't want to know that because then you would have to feel some of his pain. We're all so wrapped up in our own minor burdens; we never stop to realize how badly other people have it.

Instead of wasting time moaning and groaning, try listening to others' stories. It will make them feel better and help them through their losses. People think just because they have money or mingle with a certain crowd, that's what makes life great. Well nothing could be further from the truth. Life really isn't that way. What goes around is a guarantee to come back around. Sure you get a kick out of making fun of bums, but what if it was you? It could happen!

www.ingramcontent.com/pod-product-compliance
Lightning Source LLC
Chambersburg PA
CBHW032214040426
42449CB00005B/587